Sissy Husband Stories

By: Mistress Jessica

First Edition
Copyright 2013

☐

The Day I Found Out About His Secret

The day that I found out my husband liked wearing female underwear was a changing point in our marriage. I still loved him very much he was a good provider for the household, but things were going to have to change as part of the acceptance of this new bit of information.

I called him out on it when he got home from work that day and he got down on his knees and begged me to understand that it was just something that had always been part of who he was. I made him beg until the tears were streaming down his face, and then he said the magic words that any good dominating wife loves to hear.

"Honey I will do anything"

I stopped him right there and asked him to make certain that he knew what he was saying, and he repeated it.

"I will do anything you want me to"

I had him get undressed right there in front of me and sure enough he was wearing pretty pink lacey underwear and black thigh highs.

He stood before me much less the man that I had married, I had thought of him as powerful and strong and masculine, but now I thought of him as something else. He was much less of a man, his cock was still rock hard but in my eyes it no longer looked big and powerful, it was smaller weaker, less worthy of my pussy.

"Get back down on your knees"

He complied with this order quite easily, and then I started to inform him of some other orders as well.

"Since you seem to want to be part of the female side of life then I think it is time you started to take on a larger amount of responsibilities around the house, from now you will be in charge of cleaning the whole house once a week, this includes doing all the laundry and ironing as well. We will work on your cooking skills as time goes by."

He nodded his head accepting my power over him.

"You will continue to wear panties and stockings but you can now move them from whatever secret hiding spot you have them in and place them in your appropriate drawers in the bedroom, and you can remove you male attire and throw it out, you will be wearing more feminine things and you will be doing it full time now."

He found this to be very scary, and you could actually see the cold chill run up his spine.

"Later today I am going to go to the store and get some shall we say new toys to fit your new position in the household, those being a butt plug, a strap on, and a chastity device."

I continued.

"You will no longer get to play the man of the house, for you are certainly no longer that. I am going to humiliate you in front of your friends, and I am going to abuse you in front of mine, eventually the whole world will find out about whom you really are and you are going to accept that."

I knew I had him and there was no place for him to go.

"So for starters, I am going to call someone to come over and fuck me, since your little panty ass is not worthy to fuck, and while I am doing so you can come closer and practice your pussy licking skills."

I watched as he scooted on his knees between my open legs, his head ducked underneath my skirt and I felt his tongue touch my clitoris. Picking up his cell phone I called one of his friends who lived close by.

"Hey Mark, yes things are ok, how are you? Good to hear it. I was wondering if you could swing by the house I need you to do something for me. No he is busy right now and can't come to the phone. Ok will see you in a little while."

While we waited for Mark to arrive I made sure he continued to lick my pussy I wanted it nice and wet, I had to admit he was good at licking pussy, and looking down at him in his predicament made me even hotter, I came two times before I heard the doorbell ring.

"Come on in I yelled"

Mark opened the door and as he entered the room he stopped in his tracks. Then he realized it was his friend who wearing the panties and stockings and not a second girl that was between my legs.

"What the hell is this" he said.

"It appears my husband and your friend prefers to wear girl things instead of stepping up and being the man that he should be. As such I have banned his little girly dick from my pussy, so I was hoping you might be able to help me out and at the same time show him what he just gave up to wear panties and stockings."

Mark looked a little apprehensive at first looking at his friend in a very different light.

"Is this ok with you" he asked him.

I watched to see what he would do and as he nodded his head I knew there would be no power struggle that he had succumbed to his new place in this relationship.

I had him go over and undo Mark's pants while my fingers showed Mark what the prize was for letting my husband be even more humiliated. As Marks manhood was revealed I was almost taken back myself, Mark had a huge cock that was dangling in front of my husband's face.

"Go ahead and touch it, I told him. Stroke it, I want to see you stroking another man's cock, I want you to feel it grow in your hands. I want you to think about yourself and how humiliating it is to be making another man's cock hard so that he can fuck your wife."

My pussy was soaking wet as Mark's cock got even bigger in my husband's hands.

"Now look up at Mark and tell him that you want him to fuck your wife."

Mark looked down at my sissy husband and I watched as the words left my husband's mouth.

"Please Mark use your big cock and have sex with my wife, make her cum over and over again."

Then I made him kiss Mark's balls as the final act of humility. Mark didn't waste no time after that with my legs high in the air he took his big cock and laying the head right under my clit, then he simply slide that monster into my wet pussy. I had never been fucked by a cock so big in my life. I watched as my sissy husband still on his knees watched his friend slide in and out of me.

"You see what you gave up when you stopped being a real man and became a sissy. I think I am going to have to get to know more of your friends a little more intimately. I had to focus on my own position as Mark's cock was going to make me cum in a way I had not cum ever. The length of Mark's cock was so much bigger then my sissy husbands, it was touching places in my pussy that I didn't even know existed. Mark's thrusts were powerful and I could feel his balls slapping up against me so I knew he was very deep inside of me, I would glance over every so often to see the tears in my sissy husbands eyes as he watched his wife get ravaged from his friend. Mark understood that this was not love making that this was hard core sex and my tight pussy from lack of big cock was soon going to cause his own eruption. When I heard him say he was going to cum, I thought for a second and then responded.

"Come on Mark, cum in my pussy give my sissy husband a nice cream pie to clean up."

With that said Mark didn't hold back at all and he began to start cumming he pulled his cock out a little and came all over my crotch and down my pussy lips.

I didn't waste a second but swung my legs around and presented my husband with a new duty he would have to perform. My pussy was covered in Mark's cum, and I was surprised to hear Mark speak down to him.

"Go on you little sissy cum drinker, I want to see you lick my cum from your wife's pussy."

He looked up at Mark and then at me and then slowly moved forward and was scooping loads of cum up off of my crotch with his tongue and his mouth got full of Mark's cum and then I watched as he swallowed it. I almost came from just that, but then his tongue was in my pussy for real hunting down all of Mark's cum and some of my own as well and that last orgasm was the best of all.

A Wife and Her Friends

My husband is so special to me, he really is, when we having a pool party and the drinks were flowing my girlfriends and I were all drinking a little too much and the boys were sitting around talking about football or something like that. We all walked over to them and in our most sexy walk, and announced we wanted to paint there toenails, all the guys were like no way, but my husband raised his hand in eagerly, all the other guys looked at him like he just caught the plague. The five of us took him by the arm and walked him away and into the bedroom. The guys went on talking about football, and whether or not my husband was really gay for wanting to have his toes painted. Inside the bedroom though we tossed him on the bed and two girls held him down with their big tits bouncing in his face, even I could see how hard there nipples were. He gave the usual feigned regret for making the decision to allow this and moved his feet around as two other girls tried to hold his legs down so I could paint his toes. I think he knew what he was doing as the two girls on his legs were holding his legs against their chest, in other words against their tits. Finally they had him, I took my time making sure to do a good job, and when I was done I pointed out to the girls holding his legs that his cock was rock hard, they all had a good laugh. I then explained we can't send him back out to the boys with painted toes and a hard on. They took the hint and two girls holding his legs pulled his bathing suit down releasing his very hard cock and went to work as I watched them run their lips up and down the side of his cock and kissing each other when they got to the head of it. It didn't take very long for one of the other girls to have her bottoms off and was straddling my husband's face and from her reaction his tongue must have went right to work. Back at his cock one girl was taking him deeply into her throat while the other one was sucking on his balls. Now I knew just how well my husband could lick a pussy and it didn't take very long before the first girl was cumming and reluctantly got off his face so the second girl who was already fingering herself was able to get on this new wonderful ride they discovered. Before he could get the second girl off though he himself was shooting his load into my best friend's mouth that in turn snowballed his load into the girl who was helping to suck his cock.

We got him cleaned up and his bathing suit was put back on and made him promise not to say a word about what just happened and then pushed him back out on to the porch with his bright red toes. Right before I closed the door he could obviously see that we were not done touching each other and all of the girls were on the bed naked and ready for more.

Out on the porch he told me later the guys looked at his toes and everything changed, they asked why he did it and stuff like that, but they all put some distance between him and them as if they didn't want to be associated with someone with possible masculine issues. The rest of the party was not very much fun for my husband but I think he was ok with it as the other guys didn't get there cock sucked off by their friends wives and girlfriends.

I found out later about further issues later as my husband stopped getting calls about things going on with his friends, who were obviously not his real friends. It was because of that reason I decided to have a party and only invite my girlfriends. I had my husband stay in the bedroom while I prepared the room; he was watching some television in the bedroom while the party went on. He was still rather distraught about his friends abandoning him like they did and I had a surprise for him.

I knew eventually he would have to come out of the bedroom to get a drink from the kitchen and I had the girls ready for him when he did.

I heard the door open and he peeked out I let him get to the kitchen and then my friends started in.

"Hey I thought this was a girl only party" she said.

Another girl replied "I know this isn't right, why is he in the house, this is only girl time."

"I think if he is going to stay he has to let us make him into a girl" said my best friend who had sucked him off at the pool party.

It only took about a minute before they dragged my husband back into the living room and began to strip off his clothes; they all giggled at him when they saw his pink toe nails which meant he had removed the red nail polish and allowed new nail polish to be added.

So the girls held him down as some went to the bathroom to get the tools needed and others went to find some clothes for him.

They proceeded to shave his legs, well they got a little excited and shaved his whole body, then they put lotion all over his body, I had to stop one girl who already had three fingers up his ass, I explained we weren't ready for that yet, but I appreciated her creativity.

Now that he was smooth as a young girl they began, evidently he didn't realize how prepared I was and when we held him down and pierced both his ears with the piercing gun from the mall I borrowed putting in two diamond earrings he looked at me with real fear in his eyes.

They proceeded to do his makeup for him and panties were chosen along with stockings and a bra, we added to the bra to make him appear to be voluptuous. When we were done I was very happy and actually surprised at how much he did look like a girl, in fact he looked really hot.

Of course his cock was sticking out and causing a tent to occur in the dress he was wearing, my best friend jumped on that as she stuck her head under his dress and by the look on his face she was doing an immediately good job and it didn't take very long before his eyes rolled into the back of his head.

We continued the party now only this time my husband was allowed to stay, he seemed amazed at the things we spoke about everything from penis sizes, how we like to be fucked and even some of the girls began making out with each other as we played truth or dare. When one of the girls took out a strap on from her purse, the girls began lining up across the couch with their asses in the air and she stepped into the strap on and began to give each of them a very good fucking. The look on my husband's face was priceless. After all those who wanted to get fucked had their chance, I brought up that I think it would be a good idea for the newest girl to get a chance and everyone agreed my husband didn't actually agree but he didn't really have much of a choice as my friends turned him around and I raised his dress and the girl with the strap on pulled his panties down, the strap on touched his anus and he clenched his ass, a few smacks on his cheeks got them relaxed again and then the strap on was pushing its way into his asshole. The girls loved it, as they began to talk about how they would love to put a plastic cock up their own husband's ass so he could understand what it is like to be penetrated. We cheered the girl with the strap on as she began to fuck my husband in earnest. Reaching down beneath his dress I felt his cock and it was hard, I announced that he must like it because his clit is rock hard again. They all laughed at how funny it was that his cock got hard while being fucked in the asshole. We flipped him over and someone new went to work on his cock. This second orgasm made him shutter as the girl continued to suck even after he shot his load into her mouth.

It was then announced that the new girl rule should be enforced. I had forgotten about that rule and it was evidently unanimous so I explained to my husband that as the new girl he would have to lay on the ground and lick all of us to an orgasm. They pulled him down to the ground and took turns straddling his face it took a while about an hour and for his efforts and accomplishments in getting us all off, another girl sucked his cock until it was hard again and I think the third time he came it actually hurt, which I thought was very funny myself.

They party thinned out and they told the new girl my husband how great he / she was and she was welcome at all of our parties now.

We got into the bedroom and my husband sat down on the edge of the bed still in his dress and makeup, I went to the bathroom to get ready for bed, and when I came out wearing a strap on, the look on his face was priceless.

"I like the fact that you took it up the ass like a good girl, now get your panty ass up on the bed so I can have some fun with your ass."

These days my husband doesn't even have male friends for the most part, but he regularly hangs out with my friends sometimes even without me, if they need someone to go shopping or to the salon and I am busy he will always stand in for me.

He has his own wardrobe of outfits that his new girlfriends have picked out for him, and he is always a hit at our parties. He has fucked every one of his former friend's girlfriend and wives and thinking back to that pool party and how much fun those other guys missed out on.

Meeting the Perfect Woman (part 1)

I was never much of a pussy growing up but I was never much of a macho guy either, the fact was I was submissive though I didn't know it at the time, but during the course of my teenage years I realized I was very much attracted to strong women, these women would want their way and I would give it to them. It was unfortunate that these women or I should really say girls were also very selfish and not well experienced so even though they got what they wanted from me they didn't understand exactly what I was capable of giving to them and eventually they saw me as a wimpy guy. The fact of the matter was that most of these girls weren't dominant at all, or strong for that matter most of them were just acting out hoping to find a guy who would take control of them and put them in line, they didn't realize that they were submissive too looking for a strong hand. Eventually I just stopped looking it wasn't really worth the effort to be continuously let down time after time, thinking that I had found someone who could truly take ownership of me only to feel neglected because the girl couldn't understand her own feelings and what it was that she herself wanted.

Sure there were some good times during it all, it was also a time when I learned how erotic humiliation could be such a turn on, who would have thought that being embarrassed or doing something so out of character could give me such a raging hard on. Of course this just complicated the matter even further how was I going to find strong women who was into humiliating the man she loved, I might as well start playing the lottery at this point seeing as I had better odds at winning that then finding a successful relationship.

It was a few years later when I met Jennifer, she was a very attractive women, she had very nice breasts, they were very perky and she had the most beautiful heart shaped ass I had ever seen. We had met at the gym I was working out on a machine that she wanted to use and she walked right up to me and said. "Get off the machine I want to use it now". I stopped immediately and got off the machine, she threw her towel at me and told me to wipe it down, and I did just that while she waited and when it was clean and dry I simply stood next to her while she did her exercises and when she was done she got off smiled at me and walked away. I watched her walk away her beautiful ass in those tights, right when she got to the next piece of equipment she turned and saw me staring at her ass, I quickly turned away but it was too late, she turned and came back over to me and in a loud voice said, "Were you staring at my ass while I was walking away from you", and then she slapped me across the face quite hard and everyone turned and looked towards us. I was so embarrassed, I turned beet red, and my spandex shorts revealed something else my cock was rock hard. I had to do extra reps while I waited for my cock to calm down. The next time I was at the gym Jennifer again kicked me off the machine I was on, when she was done she told me to get her a cup of water, of course I immediately went and did that for her, she had moved to another machine and I stood next to it until she was done and handed her the cup of water, she drank it all in one shot and told me to get her another one. I immediately did just that, and when I returned I stood to the side as Jennifer was having a conversation with another lady. "I don't care how good in bed a man is, if he isn't willing to do what I tell him he isn't worth my time at all", she then turned and saw me standing there. "Take a look at this guy, I caught him staring at my ass the other day and now he will do anything I ask him to do." The other girls snickered as I stood there with the cup of water, she took it from my hands and with her free hand pulled open my spandex shorts and poured the cup of water down them. The wet spot it made looked like I peed on myself, the girls all started to laugh but not Jennifer, she looked at me with a serious face. "Now go finish your workout and you better do every single machine like you always do". I walked away but could still hear them snickering at my demise, of course there were a few other comments from the guys about not being able to hold my fluids and stuff, got some more laughs from them. It wasn't until the next day that I realized why she had me do the full workout, my crotch was rubbed raw and though I couldn't workout the next day I still showed up to the gym anyway. Jennifer saw me walk in and called me over, "I am very glad you showed up today, because if you hadn't I would have known that you were not truly ready to give yourself completely to me, we are going out to dinner this evening here is my address pick me up promptly at seven". Then she reached in her bag and pulled out a small bag and told me not to look in the bag until I got home that it was a gift and that I should wear them tonight for her. The ride home was took forever, my mind was racing trying to deduce what it was that was in the bag, but I did not have enough information, I parked the car and raced into the house and into the bedroom, dumping the bag onto the bed I was taken aghast at what I saw there.

Upon the bed was a pair of black stockings, a black garter belt, and a pair of crotch less panties also black. Next to that pile was a bottle of hair removal cream, and also a bright Pink Butt Plug. I was about to freak out when I realized that there was a note in the bag as well.

It read…

"Now I noticed how your cock became hard when I ordered you around at the gym, so I am going to make the leap and assume you are a submissive person and enjoy a strong woman that takes charge of her man, the fact that you continued your work out even after I made it look like you took a leak in your shorts showed me that you enjoy humiliation which to tell you the truth is one of my favorite things to do to a submissive man. With that said I am taking a chance on you, I don't normally do this sort of thing, as I am a very private person but you intrigued me and that doesn't happen very often. The one thing that I have wanted was a man who for lack of a better term is willing to be my little sissy bitch, one of the things that is required is that he be willing to dress up as a sissy bitch and do exactly what I say. I am hoping you are that kind of man, if you are then I will expect you at my house at six instead of seven and obviously dressed pretty without any hair on your body at all except your head, I like my man smooth and silky. Do not put the butt plug in but bring it as a gift to me and allow me the honor of plugging you for the first time. If on the off chance I am totally wrong about you then do what you want with the things in the bag but never speak to me or look at me again else I will bring you up on charges. Hope to see you at six."
I re-read the note three times, I couldn't believe what it said, and picking up the garter and the stockings they were so silky and smooth. I picked up the bottle of hair remover and looked at the clock, my clothes were off and I was in the shower reading the directions on how to use this product.

I applied a healthy dose of the product to every part of my body and stood still in the shower as my skin began to tingle, and the tingling soon became an itch, it was driving me crazy, but I had to stand the itch for another seven minutes for maximum effect. When it was ready I used the little plastic thing that came with the package and each time when I scrapped it across the cream what was left behind was skin so smooth it was like it was brand new. It took about another ten minutes but when I emerged from the shower I was without hair below my neck and my body felt more alive than it had in a long time.

I arrived at her house at six on the dot, and rang the doorbell when she opened the door she was dressed amazingly, she was wearing a short cocktail dress with fishnet stockings and very high heels, she opened the door and let me into her home. I entered and offered her the pink butt plug as she had told me to do, and she smiled. "I was so glad I was right about you, now go into that room and drop your trousers and lay on the bed."

I entered her bedroom and unbuckled my pants letting them fall around my ankles, the stockings and made my legs feel amazing, I laid face down on the bed my ass was so exposed in the panties, hearing her enter the room, I could tell she was standing behind me. I heard the snap of surgical gloves and then I felt her fingers probing my anus, one finger then two, the cream she used was very cold, her fingers withdrew and she tossed the pink butt plug on the bed in front of me. The plug itself really wasn't that big, it was almost cute, I could see her come around to the end table and what she withdrew was much more intimidating, it was a much bigger plug and it was black. She turned and smiled at me, and said "Yes I think this one will do much more nicely" I watched her walk out of my vision to stand behind me and then I felt the beginning s of the plug being pushed into me. The tip of it wasn't so bad and she was moving it in slowly, but that started to change and the pressure behind the plug became increasingly stronger my anus screamed out as it was stretched further and further allowing entry of this foreign invader into my asshole. Once I overcame the crest of the device it simply slipped into place, locked in a place, suspended between fully inside of me and fully outside of me. I stood a little awkward at first but better in a minute or two, pulling my pants up Jennifer smiled at me. "I truly like a man that is not afraid to be penetrated by a woman, which is just the start of things like that if this goes the way I think it will."

We arrived at the restaurant and after sitting down, the waiter came to her and not to me, I guess he was familiar with her, and she told him that she would like a glass of wine and that I would like a Shirley Temple. The waiter smirked at her and left, I was confused but at the same time embarrassed normally I would have ordered my own drink but she was in charge now and I went with it. She informed me that she liked me and would very much like for me to consider being her boyfriend, she continued to explain the rules of that even when the waiter walked up, which was very embarrassing as she was discussing the fact that I was not going to be allowed to fuck her at first. "Yes we are very to order, I would like to have the New York Strip steak and he would like to have the Cobb salad." The waiter thanked her and removed himself. "Now like I was saying you may consider me your girlfriend but you should know that I have other lovers and I am not going to stop enjoying myself just because I have a boyfriend. In addition you may or may not be part of certain activities if they happen to be at my house when you are there. Now even though you are in good shape you are going to have to lose some additional weight specifically around your waist, I am not going to go out and buy another wardrobe for you to wear when some of my older clothes would be sufficient so until you can fit into my clothes you are officially on a diet." I was at a loss of how exciting it was to be totally under her control, Jennifer was everything that I had always wanted, and the fact that she took it to an even higher level was like heaven on earth. I felt her barefoot come up under the table and she felt to see if my cock was hard and it was raging. "Good I am glad to see that you approve, a few more details, from now on you will only wear panties and stockings so when you go home tonight I will give you another bag, you will throw all of your old things away. You are to keep yourself hairless, and have you ever sucked a cock before?" I was caught off guard by the question at first; I mentioned I had a bisexual experience in college. "How big was his cock?"

she asked. It was of average length I think, maybe five or six inches I told her. "No, that simply will not do, I don't fuck average men and I certainly don't want you gagging on their large cocks, we will have to work on that." Again I was aghast at what she was saying and couldn't believe it, this woman was going to take over my life and I was so looking forward to it.

She only allowed me to finish half of the salad before she told me I was not allowed to eat anymore; she however continued to enjoy her steak until she had finished the whole thing. I also got to sit and watch her enjoy desert and coffee.

When we arrived back at the house she instructed me to disrobe of everything that made me a man to the world. She then took me into the bedroom and pushed me between her legs, she did not have any panties on and she simply said, "make me cum" and I knew this was another test so I did my best and was able to make her cum with just my tongue, she seemed very happy about this. When she was satisfied she made her way off of the bed and back to the end table, withdrawing what looked a bunch of belts with a ring on one end she stepped into what became a strap on harness. She pulled out assorted dildo's that could attach to the device and she decided on one that was about eight inches long and very thick, she told me that this was a mold of the penis of her smallest lover, and until such time as I could prove my worthiness to her it would be me on the receiving end.

My legs were up in the air as Jennifer removed the plug which was even more amazing then when it went in the first time, and my gaping asshole was soon filled with a very large and thick rubber cock which Jennifer drove into me fully on the first push. I couldn't believe I was lying on a bed in stockings being fucked by the most beautiful woman I knew. She fucked me for about twenty minutes telling me what a good sissy bitch I was going to be, when she started playing with my cock, her fingers were so firm wrapped around my shaft, and it didn't take very long before cum was shooting out of the head of my cock and landing on my face. Jennifer stopped fucking me and she looked at my cum covered face with such admiration, she released my cock and wiped the cum on my face into my own mouth, and I sucked the last drop off of her finger.

She agreed that the date had gone very well, and that she was satisfied that I could be the man that she wanted in her life, she went into her closet and brought out another skirt she called it a pencil skirt and told me to get dressed in it, it slid up nicely and it held my legs together as well, it was very sexy, she handed me a bra, telling me I might as well get used to wearing that as well, I didn't think nothing about it, and then a blouse. After putting all these things on she told me that I was too go home dressed like this, I informed her I had taken the subway train to her house but she didn't care, when she gave me the high heel shoes I started to get a little scared.

She ushered me out of the house giving me a little jacket to help keep me warm and there I was walking down the street dressed fully as woman on the first night I had ever even played at it. The train ride was very scary as some people realized what I was and some didn't care as they came on to me. I truly understood what a despicable species men really are after that train ride, I truly thought that we men didn't deserve to wear the pants in the family, and when I told Jennifer about the incident and how I felt she was very glad to hear this, and she informed me that I would never ever wear the pants again.

Meeting the Perfect Woman (part 2)

For the next few weeks I would arrive at Jennifer's house dressed as a man, and upon entering I would change into my female clothing and go about doing the house work and cleaning the floors, doing laundry folding and ironing all of Jennifer's clothing, she liked to have things put away just right.

For lunch I would serve her a wonderfully prepared meal on the porch I of course would stand next to her to assist her with anything she required. She had me standing now in five inch heels which still made walking a little difficult and my feet would be so sore by the end of the day, I complained a few times about them and she whipped my ass until I had tears ruining my makeup running down my face. She didn't like to hear a man complain about what a woman goes through on a daily basis.

One time she caught me with my skirt pulled up as I was urinating into the toilet, she was very upset about this for some reason and left the house immediately I continued on about my chores and was down on the floor scrubbing it clean when she arrived back at home telling me to cease what I was doing and to follow her to the bedroom.

She never told me what it was but when she started to play around my crotch area I thought maybe she had purchased a new present for me and was all smiles as I held my skirt up exposing my smooth skinned crotch to her. She was not very gently as I felt some sort of ring placed around my balls and cock, it fit very snuggly, I couldn't figure out what exactly it was but it was so rare that she played with my cock I figured I must have done something good to receive such attention. Next it felt like she was poking or pushing my cock into something. When she was satisfied that everything was in place I heard a little click. "There now, I don't expect you will be doing anymore peeing standing up like a real man, from now on you will have to sit down and pee like a real girl, and best of all your punishment for even doing that will be to be locked up for a month so you can't even play with your little boy clit unless I let you." I looked down and saw that my cock was effectively locked up and when I reached down to touch it all that was there was hard plastic. "Now let us test this thing out and see if you can get an erection while wearing it" Jennifer scooted back on to the bed lifted her skirt and started to play with her clitoris, my cock instantly started to get hard, but it found itself constrained and limited in size, soon it was pushing against any opening it could find as the blood continued to rush into it and with nowhere for it to grow it bulged and pushed back into my body, it was excruciating , Jennifer thought it was a perfect punishment and laughed at my discomfort. I was dismissed and went back to working around her house.

Up till this point I had satisfied Jennifer with my tongue, she had never let me fuck her yet, and I think she was getting to the point where she was going to need a cock insider of her, she started making me fuck her with the dildo's but that wasn't enough for her, and soon I heard her on the phone as I was hanging up her lingerie in the closet. "Yes of course I miss you, how long are you in town for, only today, well you should come over and spend some of that time with me, what you are free right now, well come on over I will be waiting for you.

His name was Tom, and when I answered the door he simply pushed by me telling me to get my little sissy ass out of his way. He didn't stop or anything just went immediately to Jennifer's room and shut the door. I was mopping the room just outside of Jennifer's room and could hear Jennifer screaming in ecstasy, he was obviously fucking her, and from the sounds of it she was enjoying the hell out of it. He must of fucked her for about an hour or so when thinks finally started to quiet down in her room. I had completed my chores and was sitting on the couch waiting for Jennifer to have something else for me to do or to send me home. During that time I looked at my new accessory and thought to myself I can't even play with myself when I get home now, and she had said I would be locked up for a month, a whole month before I would get any release, I started to sob a little from the depression of it all as it finally swarmed over me and what I had become. The door suddenly opened and Tom came out naked with his cock dangling there in front of him. He walked over and told me to stand up and then asked to see my new toy. I started to hesitate when he grabbed my arm roughly telling me he would not ask again. Slowly my slender arms lowered down to the hem of my skirt and my fingers gingerly curled around the hem and raised my skirt up to expose my crotch. He looked at it bent over for a closer look and then knocked on the hard plastic that surrounded my cock as if he was knocking on a door. The bellow of his laughter could be heard by the neighbors. I felt so embarrassed which of course started to make my cock hard again which it found no release for causing me again a level of un comfort that I was sure to be my life moving forward. Tom stood back up and told me that Jennifer has requested my presence, as I turned to walk towards Jennifer's room Tom swatted me on the ass and it stung, he laughed again looking at what he thought was such a pathetic man in a skirt. I entered Jennifer's room seeing her naked on the bed all sweaty and I thought something was wrong, and ran as best I could in the high heels to her bedside. I asked her if she was ok, if Tom had hurt her, she smiled at me. "You are such a good sissy, here I was having sex with another man instead of you and you are concerned if I was ok, you are the most amazing man I have ever met." She smiled at me and it lit up my whole inside knowing how much she cared about me. "My sweet little sissy, Tom left me full of his cum and I want you to get between my legs and clean me up" She pointed at her crotch which was covered in sweat and sticky cum from where Tom must have dripped after pulling out of her pussy. "Be a good sissy and lay on the bed and I will sit on your face so you can get all of Tom's cum at one time." As I lay on the bed and watched her swing her sweaty leg over my face her pussy which was red and swollen from the fucking she just had slowly lowered itself until it was right over my mouth, and I could see the cum gathering at her opening it was like looking out onto a snowy yard during the winter time, nothing but white, and in as it over came the last things that held it back it simply flowed out of her pussy and into my awaiting mouth, swallowing that first load of another man's cum was the most disgusting thing I had ever done, it was bad enough when she made me lick my own cum up but this was some other guy's load of cum. My cock was again bulging at the sides of its cage and it hurt. All that was left now was to lick up the residue from Tom that was still inside of her and all over her crotch. Jennifer was so happy with my performance that she said I had done all of my chores and that I could go home. As always she had already picked me out something to go home in, it was like a sweater dress that only came down to about mid-thigh and if I wasn't careful I would expose my stockings and garter.

I was just about ready to leave when Jennifer comes up to me and reaches up my skirt pulls my panties to the side and pulls out the butt plug she has had me been wearing each time I come over to her house. "When you are taking the train home if anyone comes on to you I want you to let them" When I heard these words it scared the shit out of me. I started to say something but she cut me off. "You will do anything that they want but it has to be on the train, it is late so maybe you will get lucky and no one will be on the train, but maybe three or four guys might decide they like the way you look and gang fuck you right there. Either way I will want to know all about it when I see you next.

When I stepped onto the train dressed rather upscale for using public transportation, I was scared as a school girl. My hair had grown a little bit and I now styled it more like a woman then a man, I got some crap about that at work but that soon faded as things often do. There was only one other person in the train car. I thought to myself, nothing was going to happen, this was public transportation, there would be people around, and I just had to make it to my stop.

There was a homeless guy sitting on the other side of the train but he seemed harmless. I kept my eyes down and my legs closed. The homeless guy was looking at me, kind of eyeing me up and down. "So what's a pretty girl like you taking the subway home late at night, are you some type of prostitute or just some lost girl looking for a good time." I wasn't going to answer him but I told him I was neither thank you. The mere fact that I acknowledged him there when I was certain most people did not was enough for him to continue the conversation and of course he said something that put me in a bad place. "Why don't you come over here and sit next to me and you could tell me all about it while you jerk me off, haven't had a pretty lady play with my cock in a long time." With that I was sunk, I slowly stood up and sat next to him as he undid what he called pants, his cock was as dirty as the rest of him and the mere fact that my hand was reaching out to touch it made me feel dirty as well, this was not what Jennifer had in mind I was sure jerking off homeless guys, I am sure she would have rather I had gotten gang banged by a bunch of hoodlums. His cock was now hard as my fingers closed around it and he closed his eyes as I began to go up and down his cock with my hand. It was a little bit bigger than average nothing at all the size of Tom's cock, Tom's cock was huge, I was surprised to see Jennifer even able to walk after Tom was done with her. I started to laugh, here I was a guy dressed up as a girl with a chastity belt locked on his own cock, jerking off some homeless guy on the train ride home fantasizing about what it was like to be fucked by Tom.

I heard the homeless guy's breath change and felt him rise a little in his seat and then his cum was running down my fingers back into the black coarse hair that surrounded his cock. He tucked it back into what once were pants, and I wiped my hands on a napkin I had in my bra throwing it away onto the floor. The homeless guy got off at the next stop and I still had a ways to go. The next voice I heard scared the crap out of me, it was right behind me and it told me not to turn around. It sounded familiar but I couldn't immediately place it. I want you to put both of your hands on that bar up above your head, I immediately complied, I felt my dress slowly inching up it was past my stockings and was at the base of my panties. "I so enjoyed looking at your ass up in the air while you were licking my load of cum out of you Mistress's pussy, I thought maybe I would like to get a piece of that pathetic sissies ass on the way home and seeing as how we both took the same train its late there is no one else here, now is as good a time as any.

With my ass now exposed for the public if there would have been any public, I heard the noise of his zipper being pulled down and felt his hardening cock flop onto the crack of my ass. "I sure hope there was still some lubricant in your asshole from when Jennifer pulled that butt plug out of your ass before you left, because I am sorry sissy I didn't bring any with me." With that said I felt him maneuver his cock in line with my asshole, and I started to pray that he was right it felt like there might still be some in there, and the head of his cock began to press against my opening. My asshole was still affected by the plug recently removed so the head of his large cock was able to easily push it back open; it was the large and long shaft of his cock that my asshole would not be used to at all. I felt his hands grab my hips and he grabbed me roughly holding me as he drove his large cock into my ass. It was the most amazing feeling in the world. I mean Jennifer's strapons that she had fucked me with before were one thing, but to have such a man as Tom, fucking me like I was some street slut on the train, my own cock was straining beyond belief against its own bonds. The thrusting continued as I felt his hips crash into my behind each time rocking my world as I held on to the bar above my head, the trains wheels were screeching as we drove through one of the stops, I could see people standing on the platform as we drove by at a slower pace and they could see me being fucked by a large man, the whole world could see me as again he drove his large phallus into my sissy ass. My own cock was bouncing around cage and all so everyone would know I was a sissy getting fucked in the train. The fucking continued for three more stations with us stopping at the third one, Tom didn't seem to even notice as a few people got on board he continued to ram his cock into my ass, those people seeing what was going on slowly backed out and went to the next car, though they came back to the door between trains to continue to watch the show.

I knew my stop was coming up next and Tom was still pounding away, about half way to my stop, the pounding of my ass changed it was quicker now and as we entered my stop, Tom shot his load into my ass, I felt it surge to fill me up. The train came to a stop and Tom pulled my dress back down and escorted me off the train to one of columns on the station and placed me against it and got back on the train. I was in no condition to move yet, I had cum dripping out of my ass and down my leg, and the front of my own dress was stained with my own cum that had shot out during the climax even locked in a chastity device I had found a way to cum, I was dripping in it as the train moved away and Tom waved goodbye. It took me a few minutes before my legs worked again especially in heels and I slowly made my way up the stairs to the street level, as I did I passed some guy going down probably getting ready to go to work and I heard him mutter under his breath "Slut" and it brought a smile to my face, I felt like a slut right then and there and for some odd reason I was very happy about it.

When I finally got to my apartment I called Jennifer and told her everything that happened, she was so happy to hear that I enjoyed it all and was she very excited now about the possibilities. I was a little confused but still elated at the night I just had and didn't think about what Jennifer was referring to at all, after all I would do whatever she asked me to do because I was hers and she loved me for who I was or I should say who she was making me into.

It Was My Birthday

It was my birthday, another year had gone by and I was another year older, life was not as good as I had thought it would be. I worked my way up the office ladder, and was now making a nice salary, but I was still deeply in debt because of student loans, and new cars, and a house and all those things that were supposed to be the American dream. Yeah I was living that alright, chasing the all mighty dollar, trying to keep the wolves at bay; all this stress was playing havoc on my life. I had bill collectors up my ass all the time, they called my house, and they called me at work. I was so upset all the time, I would bite and growl at anyone who would interrupt me when I was doing something; this pushed my friends and my neighbors away quite easily. I hadn't realized it but it also pushed my wife away from me. I didn't notice it at first; we still made love on a regular basis, though I started to feel that she wasn't that much into the whole thing. To me it was a way to relax shooting my cock off was about the only thing that I had left to me.

The day that I received the letter from the law firm about some debt I owed was the last straw, that night when I went to fuck my wife to try and have some relief my cock wouldn't even work. My wife rolled over and went to sleep, I tried to get it to work but it wouldn't, I was sitting there with my dick in my hand when my wife woke up. I guess I was making too much noise or something and she rolled over and looked at me with my cock in my hand, and began to laugh at me. "What is the matter is your little boy dick not working anymore, what did you do miss a payment on that one too." I was so pissed, I mean I was about to go in a rage.

"Don't get angry at me it's not my fault your little dicklet doesn't work anymore"
She continued.
"Maybe you play with it too much; maybe I should lock your little puny cock up"
"Would you like that, then maybe I would get a good fucking every once and awhile."
She was degrading me humiliating me it should have made me take my hand off of my cock, but I kept playing with it.
"If you weren't so caught up in chasing the money all the time, maybe you would have noticed that I am fucking your boss and your best friend and they have cocks so much bigger than yours, they know how to make me cum."
I didn't look down but looked at her as she continued.
"You are such a worthless piece of crap, I would divorce your ass if I could but you even ruined that you stupid little prick"
"You are so dumb, that I fucked Larry your best friend while you were at the gym, my pussy is still filled with his cum, and you are such a pussy sitting there with a hard on to do anything about it."
Then she stopped and we both looked down at my cock, it was rock hard and I mean rock hard. We looked at each other and then she moved to get on my cock. I felt my hard cock slide into her cum filled pussy as she rode my cock I could see Larry's cum covering my cock each time she slid up and down on my cock. I flipped her over on the bed and fucked her missionary position. Every time I felt my cock becoming limp she would start in again.
"Do I need to get Larry over here to finish the job again; I might as well put you in panties and make you into my little sissy bitch"
At that my cock jumped up again and I was back in the groove, the next move was hers and she pushed me over climbing back on top again.
"Come you little sissy, shoot your little cocks load in me, let me feel your sissy cum drool out of your puny little cock."

I could feel myself getting close.

"Tomorrow I am going to buy you a pair of panties and a bra, because you are not a real man like Larry and your boss is, you are nothing but a little panty wearing sissy husband."

I was getting closer each and every time she spoke.

"I can't wait to tell Larry and your Boss once I get you into panties what a little sissy faggot you are"

And with that I felt my balls start pumping and pumping and it was the best orgasm I ever had, nothing mattered at that moment, the bills, the lawyers, not even the fact that my wife was cheating on me, all that mattered was the physical feeling of shooting my load into my wife and the orgasm that lingered in my head.

When I finally came around from lingering in that wonderful place, I looked up to see my wife had scooted up and now had her pussy dripping with cum over my face.

"Cum on you little sissy, you seemed to get off on be humiliated and degraded well get your tongue in there and clean me up."

Without even thinking I pulled her cum soaked pussy down on my face, my tongue slid into her vagina and was rewarded with the feeling of a load of not only my cum but evidently my best friend Larry's cum as well. I don't know what words would describe the feeling of licking a load of cum out of your wife's pussy but it was very degrading; I didn't feel like much of a man anymore. I knew my wife had truly hit the nail on the head, I was not a man, I was something less. It didn't matter what she thought of me as long as she kept doing what she did, I couldn't explain it, but listening to her put me down the way she did was the hottest thing in the whole world.

The next day when we woke up we didn't speak about anything that had happened the night before, not the things she said, or the fact that she was sleeping with my boss and my best friend. We had our breakfast and I was off to work. Things were once again like they were before and phone calls and work delays and everything else that made my day so fucking special.

When I came home I walked in and could hear my wife in the bedroom with Larry no doubt as she was screaming out to god, which was something she never did when she and I had sex. I went to the computer and turned it on and as they fucked in my bedroom, I started looking at porn.

Normally I looked at regular porn but now I started to remember some of the things she called me last night and I began to found pictures and stories and even videos about all sorts of things. I watched as wives fucked other men in front of their husbands and made them lick their lovers cum from there pussies, some even made them suck the cum on their lovers cocks. I thought that was a little much, but my cock seemed to like it because it was hard again.

My door was cracked and I turned in time to see my naked wife making out with Larry evidently thanking him for the wonderful fucking he just gave to her. Once Larry had left I heard the door to my office creak open and my wife entered and looking at what I was watching.

"Oh so you are doing a little research on your new position in the household."

She put her leg up on the desk and I scooted over and leaned in and looked at the amount of cum that was oozing down her leg. I looked up at her smile as I ran my tongue up her leg and Larry's cum just simply moved from her leg to my tongue and then into my mouth and down my throat, my wife gave me a new name right then and there, she called me her little cum dump.

"I love seeing you in this position; it is by far my favorite thing in the whole world"

I made her cum right there in my office, what I didn't see was dangling from her fingers.

"I wanted to show you what I bought for you today."

I looked up and there on her fingers was a pair of panties and a bra, they were fancy, and lacey, and bright.

"I bought you seven different pairs and in different colors and styles so you can wear a new pair each day, I have already thrown you male things away, and oh yes, I have also informed Larry and your Boss about your new position and that you will be wearing panties and a bra each day to work. They both thought it was hilarious, your boss was crying he was laughing so hard. He had a suggestion as well, that maybe I should start you on sucking cock, and then you would at least be good at something at work"

My cock was rock hard and I took her right there on my desk, and of course I cleaned her out once I was finished.

Before I left that room I was in a Bra and panties.

That first day of work was a hard one as it was obvious I was wearing a bra under my shirt, I tried to wear my jacket all day but the secretaries knew it right away. I was only grateful my boss was out for the rest of the week.

When he finally did get back into the office, it didn't take him very long to call me into his office.

"So I was speaking with your wife, and she tells me that you know that she and I are fucking and I wanted to talk to you about it."

Before I could say anything he continued.

"I don't want you to think I give a shit about what you think, I am going to keep fucking her, but I really want to see if what she told me was true."

I looked at him not understanding.

"Come on let me see, I can't believe she put you in panties and a bra, I just have to see for myself"

I couldn't believe it, but there I was standing and taking my pants and shirt off so my boss could see the bright yellow bra and panties I had on.

He laughed and laughed when I started to get dressed he stopped me. He picked up the phone and called my wife and laughed again, he then even suggested to my wife that she should have me in stockings as well. Evidently she thought this was a great idea much to my demise.

Then he was asking her something else, though I hadn't caught what he had said to her.

"Are you sure it is ok with you, I don't want to do something that would upset you or our relationship, but if you don't have a problem with it. Ok I will see you later."

When he hung up the phone he looked at me kind of funny.

"Well I am sure you heard what I asked your wife so why don't you come over here by the desk"

As I scooted closer in my bra and panties, I suddenly realized what it was that he had asked my wife.

"It seems you are going to be taking on some additional responsibilities here at the office"

And with that I watched my boss unzip his zipper and take out his very large cock and I knew nothing was ever going to be the same again.

The Car Ride on the Coast

It was one of my favorite things to do, when work and life start to get to me, I like to jump in my car and go for a ride, and not just any ride a special one up the coast. You see there is this highway that is perfect on one side you have the hills going up on the other side you have this drop off that goes to the ocean, the scenery is some of the most beautiful I have ever seen.

Work had been unbelievably difficult today and my wife was not very understanding, so I told her I was going to go for a drive. I went to the closet got my driving bag and took off, she just shook her head at me as I left and went back to doing what she was doing.

I had to make a stop before I got on the highway, when I was all set and ready I turned the radio up and turned onto the entrance ramp. The highway had to go through the city as it winded its way to the coastline and then turned north. I was driving normal the radio was playing some popular dance song as a big rig trucker slowly overtook me, he blew his big air horn which startled me and looking over he made some lewd gesture at which I smiled at and hit the gas leaving him behind.

Soon I left the city behind and was presented with open road.

Settling in as the cool coastal air whipped through my hair, I pushed the button on the radio and switched over to my favorite play list, those songs always made me want to drive fast and with the open road in front of me I pushed the gas pedal down and felt the car jump and speed up. I could feel my troubles and worries simply being blown off of me, I was finally able to start to relax, and really enjoy the day. The afternoon was gorgeous, looking out over the cliff I could see the sail boats running parallel to the coastline and the long stairways where people could walk down to the beach were slipping by like fence posts. There weren't very many cars on the road this afternoon, I couldn't have asked for a better day. Of course I knew I probably shouldn't have thought that because literally as those words drifted off into my brain I saw the flashing lights behind me.

I immediately slowed down hoping they would simply pass me by, maybe they were going after someone else, and it couldn't be me, not now, not today.

The police car positioned himself right behind my car and continued to flash his lights; the siren was overwhelming the music in my car it was like the world was crashing down all around me.

I continued down the road a ways till I came to one of those stairways going down to the beach, this one happened to be empty which I thought was a good idea with what was about to happen.

This had never happened, you would have thought that I would have been a little better prepared for something like this; I mean I did think about it before but that was because it was exciting to think about the danger of it all. I never ever thought something like this would ever happen to me, and here it was right now happening, my worst night mare.

The police car came to a stop behind me and I watched in my side mirror as he got out of the car, I was surprised to see two police officers one either side of my car. I tried my best to be calm but I was visibly shaking from my nerves just giving up on me. They were on either side of my car now, the one on my side was saying something but I couldn't hear him, I was so scared right now that I was about to faint. He repeated his statement and this time I heard him.

"I am going to need to see your license and insurance card Ma'am"

I reached over to the purse that was on my passenger seat and retrieved my license and opened the glove box and undid my seat belt and I had to reach over to find my insurance card. This action I realized was lifting my skirt far enough up my leg to reveal my garters and thigh high stockings that I had on. Leaning back over and sitting properly again I began to hand the officer the documents he requested.

All I could think about as I watched my hand extend towards the officer was that once he looked at my license and realized that I was a man that all hell was going to break loose.

He took my license and insurance card and they both walked back to the police car.

I looked at my hand and it was visibly shaking, my whole body was shaking I was close to tears.

The waiting was the hardest part, they seemed to take forever, I was wondering if they were calling my wife or my job, or who knows the news station, the longer it took the crazier my ideas of what was going to happen to me.

What felt like thirty minutes but in actuality was probably only ten I saw their car doors open as they got back out of the car and made their way to my car.

He stood right next to my car door and he was looking at my license.

Then he said.

"Ma'am I am going to need you to step out of the car"

He then opened my car door.

I slid my legs out and could only pray that I would be able to stand up in the high heels I had on, I had never walked in them when I was ever this scared before. I stepped away from the door and he closed it for me.

"I am going to need you to step around to the other side of your vehicle because of being so close to the highway it is a safety issue"

He walked behind me as I made my way around the trunk of my car and walked between my car and the police car. As I got to the other side of my car I leaned against it so I wouldn't fall down.

The two police officers were standing there in front of me.

"Ma'am your license shows a completely different picture on it then what we see before us"

I started to blurt out that I could explain that I was having some fun that I was having a very bad day and that dressing up was a way I used to relax. He stopped me.

"Ma'am by all accounts you could have stolen this car and you may have done something diabolical to the original owner as he is nowhere to be found and the car may have been reported stolen."

He continued

"Since you're a woman, we have a limited number of options available to us, one of them would be to bring you back to the precinct and have the car towed to the impound lot while we sort all this out"

I began jabbering and begging them to not arrest me that I couldn't handle that, my wife my career everything that I hold dear to me would be ruined. The tears started to well in my eyes as I watched everything start to unravel right there in front of me.

"Ma'am there is another option that is available to us."

I tried to gather my thoughts together and was able to stop crying and looked at the two officers standing in front of me. I stammered out the words. What is the second option? I asked.

"Well Ma'am option two would involve going with one of us down that stairwell so that you could demonstrate that you are what you say you are."

I didn't quite understand, but something inside of me got me off the car and I walked past the two officers and made my way towards the stairs.

The first landing was only about ten steps downward where the stairway turned and went off in another direction.

When I turned back around the other officer who hadn't said anything was coming down the stairway.

He was unbuckling his belt and I soon found myself on my knees, he still didn't say anything when he took his cock out of his pants, it wasn't hard but it was already about five inches long. I did hear him say something when I wrapped my red lips around the head of his cock.

I had been cross dressing and taking these little trips up the coast for quite a while I was pretty sure my wife knew about it but I had never done anything else then get dressed up. This was the first time I had ever had a man's cock in my mouth. It felt smooth as he slid it in and out of my mouth, it was getting hard and it was getting longer. I knew what it was that I liked when I had my own cock sucked so I tried to do just that, I made sure my teeth were not making contact with his cock, and I used my tongue underneath the head of his cock. He was being gentle with me, or at least that was the way he started off, as his cock became fully erect he began more forcibly pushing it deeper and deeper into my mouth.

I could feel my gag reflex kicking in and I knew I would be in a bad spot if I threw up on this police officers crotch. I knew I had to breathe through my nose and if I timed it right I would be able to hold my breath long enough for him to push it down my throat. Fully hard he was probably around eight inches long, and his hands were on the back of my head and I could feel him pushing me onto his cock. The head of his cock was fast approaching the back of my throat and I thought I should start swallowing giving him access to my throat and then I felt the head of his penis slip down past the back of my mouth and into my throat. I had literally swallowed his cock, he brought it back out and I gasped out loud for air. He was jerking his cock now and he was getting ready to cum I put my mouth on just the head of it and felt his cum shooting onto my tongue, it seemed like he came forever. When he was done he cupped my chin and I opened my mouth to show him his cum sitting on and around my tongue. Then I swallowed his load.

He smiled and helped me back to my feet and told me to wait right here.

The Police officer who had done the talking was next to come down the stairs. I began to lower myself to my knees and he said no and helped me back up.

He stood right in front of me and took me around the waist and began to kiss me, his tongue was in my mouth and I had not expected this, I thought he was going to want a blow job. I found my own tongue entering his mouth as we French kissed.

Then he spun me around so I was facing the ocean, his hands roamed up my chest until they found my nipples and he began to play with them. I could feel my cock start to stir and I was nervous if he saw my cock standing out. Next his hands began unbuckling his pants and soon they were around his ankles. I heard him spitting in his hand and then my skirt was up and my panties were pulled to the side. Evidently he didn't want to see my balls. The head of his cock though slightly lubricated with his spit was in no way ready to break my anal cherry, or at least thought so. The pressure he was putting between my ass cheeks was extreme and then I felt my anus start to open to him. His hands were now on my hips and I was watching a beautiful sailboat slowly making its way south. His cock may not have been as big as partners but my asshole had only ever had a finger up it every once and awhile. I was in no way prepared to receive a cock in that opening. He eventually got his cock into me and the pain of his cock going in and out of my asshole was something that I had never experienced before. All the while I was holding on to the rail of the stairwell trying to think of anything else. He was about five minutes into stealing my anal cherry when I realized that it no longer hurt and that I was actually moaning from his thrusts into my asshole. Evidently with my asshole being so tight it didn't take long before it was milking every little bit of cum his balls had stored up since the last time he blew his load.

I heard him start moaning and so was I and his thrusts were more forceful and each time it was like everything in front of me was running at a time different rate of time than normal, that last thrust as he shot his load into me, the whole world kind of wobbled.

He removed his cock from my asshole and told me to enjoy the view for about five minutes before making my way up the stairs. I nodded and he disappeared. My panties slid back over my ass and skirt fell back into place as he left and I continued to watch the sailboat making its way. I don't know how long I waited before I turned towards the way back to my car. I felt wet in my own crotch and pulling up my skirt revealed that I had also cum in my panties which was strange because I didn't remember shooting my own load, but I imagine that happened when the whole world sort of wobbled.

I got back into my car and made my way home, stopping to change back into my regular male clothing. I felt totally purged of everything good and bad, it was a very different feeling then my normal everyday car rides.

I still take that ride as often as I can, and I find myself speeding just for the sake of hoping to get pulled over, I have paid a number of speeding tickets but have never had the chance to pay off my fines in the way I did that day, still hoping to do it again though so I keep trying.

Dans Party

My Mistress was very kind to me, I was the only man in her life, well I wasn't really so much of a man, I mean she had made me into a sissy, and when I wasn't required to wear men's clothing I would be required to be fully dressed as a little slut. Most recently she had caught me masturbating and was not very happy with me because when it came time to fuck her I was unable to get hard, this infuriated her and the next day she put me into a chastity device. It was a most uncomfortable device as it prevent me not only from touching myself or providing any physical satisfaction to myself but it also prevented me from getting an erection, now you may be thinking that isn't too bad until you realize the way it does this is by holding your penis in a small space which prevents your penis from expanding to its full length, it will try but when it hits the end of the cage it starts to push back into your body, which can be painful and is always extremely uncomfortable. Mistress demonstrated this to me after clicking the lock closed by getting right in front of my face and began to play with herself. This excites me to no end, and my cock immediately sprang to life only to be shut down and me to find myself in excruciating agony which she found to be most amusing.

Now we do keep our little games to ourselves and lead a most normal type life outside of our home, nobody in the neighborhood has any idea of what we are up to behind closed doors and I am perfectly ok with that, seeing as I am the one that would look rather pathetic and be humiliated if news got out about how we conduct ourselves in our own home.

Mistress came in to the house reading a letter that the postal service had just delivered; she had a big smile on her face. She explained to me that our dear friend Dan Sutherland was having a party tomorrow night and we were invited. Dan lived in the next town north of us, and we had known him for a very long time.

We left for the party and like always I was wearing panties and stockings underneath my male casual clothing. Mistress was feeling extra special and had me plug my ass, well to be truthful she enjoys putting the plug inside of me, she knows I would do it slowly and she likes to slide it right into me in one shot, she enjoys seeing me uncomfortable both physically and psychologically. The quick expansion of my asshole as it wrapped around the plug was extremely painful but only for a second or two then it was a dull throb for about five minutes, sort of like when you sprain your ankle.

The drive over there was uneventful; well I guess that isn't really true, while I drove Mistress masturbated next to me, which of course caused me great discomfort because of the chastity device. After she came she reached over and patted my hard crotch, hard because of the plastic device encasing my cock not because I was able to get a hard on, then she laughed a good laugh at my expense.

Arriving at the party Dan met us at the door, there were about thirty people at the party, it had been so long since we had seen Dan, and we spent some time outside the house catching up. The party was in full swing and we saw some other friends and joined in conversations. I would catch Mistress from time to time flirting with a group of men, she would always know I was watching and look over at me and wink, she knew this drove me crazy, I had some jealousy issues and she would always poke fun at me over it. I guess it was normal for me to feel jealous as she was flirting with men and I being less than your average male seeing as I was wearing women's clothing more than male clothing most of the time would give pretty much any male some insecurity problems. She played on that weakness brought about by the cross dressing and how she enjoyed humiliating me, especially if she could humiliate me sexually in front of other people and they were totally unaware of it, that was one of her specialties. The party wore on till late into the night and as people drifted off back to their homes, Dan invited us to stay the night at his house. It was a little after midnight and it was now just the three of us and Mistress got up to use the restroom thinking that Dan was in his own restroom. She startled him when she opened the door; she apologized quickly and closed the door. She came sat down next to me and told me what had happened, then she told me that she had seen Dan's cock and it was very big, much bigger then my own. She was getting horny I could tell, I knew she was going to want me to fuck her this evening, and I was looking forward to being out of my chastity device. It was then that she turned to me and explained that she was very horny and that she really needed to feel a cock inside of her pussy. We began kissing and then she whispered in my ear that she had forgotten the key to the device that it was sitting on the bathroom counter. I felt my heart sink to the floor.

Dan came back in and sat down in the chair opposite from us. Mistress didn't waste any time in formulating a new plan for her own satisfaction. She turned to Dan and told him that he had a very nice size cock, that she had never known that his cock was so big. Dan blushed with embarrassment as she continued; no really your cock is huge much bigger than his cock, looking at me now I blushed with embarrassment. Dan mentioned how some women are actually scared of his cock sometimes; they think it is too big for them. Mistress smiled back and simply said well I wouldn't be one of those women that is for certain. In fact I want to show you something Dan, and she told me to stand up. I looked at her like what are you doing, but she insisted that I stand up. Without another hesitation once I was standing she began to unbuckle my belt and in another moment my pants were on the floor and there I was standing in front of one of our closest friends in pink panties and black stockings. Dan looked astonished and told Mistress that he had no idea that I was into that. Mistress explained that it was something that she discovered early in our relationship and she kind of enjoyed the fact that she was the boss of the relationship and it was like having a full size Barbie doll to play with when I was home. That and the fact that he does all the laundry and house work in a pretty French maid outfit. Dan laughed out loud at this, the humiliation was over the top and for some strange reason I could feel my cock beginning to grow.

Mistress continued the real reason I bring this all up and reveal a very long secret to you is this. She pulled my panties down and revealed my cock locked in my chastity device. Dan looked at my cock pushing against the cage and then at Mistress. She explained that she had gotten a little tipsy this evening and was extremely horny, but unfortunately she had forgotten the key to the device back at home and really needed to feel a cock inside of her pussy and after seeing how well-endowed Dan was she couldn't resist the opportunity that had presented itself to her.

Dan thought about this and appeared to be on the verge of agreeing to the whole thing when Mistress stopped. One other thing that I really want to see though is I want him to ask you, I want him to beg you, I want him to see the cock that will be fucking me, and I want him to kiss it while he is begging you to fuck me. You see I love humiliating him and we don't involve outsiders in our affairs but since this is happening I think it makes perfect sense to include his humiliation in this as well.

Dan shook his head like sure what the fuck. After I was out of my clothes I found myself at Dan's feet kneeling between his legs, and looking up at his face, this old friend of mine didn't look the same as he did before in my eyes. Then I was asking him to fuck Mistress, and then I was begging him, he stood before me and told me to undo his pants, as I slid them down it became obvious he didn't wear underwear as his large cock literally fell onto my face, it was huge like Mistress had described. It was hanging right in front of my face the shaft was touching my lips. Mistress asked Dan if it was ok if he put it in his mouth. Dan was like I think he should suck it and make me hard for you, and with that I opened my mouth and Dan one of my oldest friends slid his very large cock into my mouth, I could barely get past the head of his cock, but when my tongue and lips moved across its surface it felt smooth and silky. I used my other hand to work more of it into my mouth. I realized this was a sissy's dream to have such a large cock in my mouth so I closed my eyes and thought of myself as just another slut doing what they do best sucking cock. It didn't take very long before he was hard and simply pulled his cock out of my mouth and went to Mistress who was waiting with her legs up and open. He slid that massive cock into her wet and waiting pussy and he fucked her like she had never been fucked before, it went on for over an hour switching positions when he took her from behind Mistress had some words for me. Mostly it was about how inadequate I was and that she may keep me locked up and just visit Dan when she needed some real cock and how pretty I looked with a cock in my mouth and other derogatory statements which she thought degraded and humiliated me but in actuality really just turned me on even more and my cock was straining against the cage and my balls were becoming blue. Eventually Mistress collapsed on the couch finished from the fucking of her life, her pussy was filled with Dan's cum and thinking that would be the ultimate humiliation she motioned me over and told me to clean her. Dan's cum was thick and sticky and I could feel the globs as they went across my tongue and down my throat. It was obvious that Dan was enjoying this and when he made suggestion that Mistress should sleep with him in his bed and that I should be tied up leaning across the dining room table she jumped at the chance to add to my discomfort. So that was where I found myself as they went off to a comfortable bed, I was tied up laying across the dining room table, it was hard to fall asleep standing up like that, eventually I found myself drifting off when I heard a sound in the kitchen behind me evidently one of them was up getting a drink. Then I heard someone enter the dining room, when I felt my panties being pulled down I began to think it was Dan. When I felt the head of his hard cock pushing against my asshole I knew it was Dan and that I should probably scream out for Mistress, but the thought of him sliding his large cock into my ass actually made me feel excited. Slowly he worked his cock into my ass, I felt his hands on my hips and then I felt him push into me fully, I gasped. With the size of his cock so large even pulling out of my asshole was just as intense as him pushing back into me. Eventually he established a rhythm to it and I felt like someone was sticking a tree up my ass, but I took it as best as I could, it took him about fifteen minutes before the thrust came more quickly and with more force and then they stopped as his hands on my hips indicated he was filling my asshole with a load of his cum. He didn't even pull my panties up as his cum slowly dribbled out of my asshole and down to my ball sack. The next morning Mistress explained that she had decided they would stay the weekend instead of going home right away and then she noticed my panties and smiled at me so it looks like you had a visit from Dan last night as well. The weekend continued to be a very interesting experience, one that I will never forget.

⬜

My Wedding Day

That fact that my marriage to my wife had been arranged is in and of itself almost barbaric, but I had no idea what was to come. It was the night before my wedding and my mother and father were finishing up dinner, I was going to go out with the boys, you know one final night of freedom type thing, but my mother had said she wanted a word with me before I went out.

I was called into the reading room and I stood before my parents, my father in his usual position with his head cast downward as my mother did the talking.

"I want you to know that we take great pride in the woman we have chosen for you, she is an amazing woman who will lead you into a wonderful life." She said. It wasn't lost on me how she had mentioned that she would lead me into the future.

"Mother, I do not want to be led I want to be the leader in my household, I am not going to let my wife run my life like you did to my father. " I said rather defiantly.

She shook her head, trying not to become angry with me. She was not one to hold back her temper though.

"You will do as you are told, or by god I will take over my knee and whip you till you can't sit down." She scolded me.

I wasn't going to back down that easy, and proceeded to poke her some more with unnecessary words describing my sentiments on her controlling ways.

I never realized how fast my mother was for her age, but she was out of the chain and had me by the collar before I ever realized what was going on. I knew she always kept a stick at hand but that was usually for my father whenever he would gain some manliness she would simply beat it out of him.

She had me over the ottoman and proceeded to whip my backside a number of times when my father spoke up.

"You know you promised her you would not present him with any marks" he said.

The whipping stopped immediately

The look of disgust my mother gave my father for stopping her was literal she raised the whip to him and he curled back into the shadow of his chair.

I stood back up to face her again but this time without the defiance.

"You should know that I looked for certain aspects and though I found the ones I wanted there is much more that I found that was unexpected." She said.

She sat back down and faced me again.

"I cannot say that I am exactly the happiest with my choice in regard to that aspect, she is going to require from you things that I do not require from your father. " She continued.

"For instance you will be expected to be totally obedient to her, she is strong let me tell you and she will not take kindly to any defiance and she will beat that out of you very quickly. She does have a few fetishes that though harmless will make you feel uncomfortable I am afraid. She likes to play dress up, and is going to expect you to play this part." She told me.

"I don't understand" I told her.

"There is no easy way to say this, so I will be upfront with you. She is going to make you dress like a girl, she will put you in panties and stockings and parade you around like a little sissy, in fact that was the word she used when we were in negotiations, she is buying you as a sissy husband. She is not going to love you unless for some reason she wants children but I believe she has better breeding stock for that purpose if she so chooses." She concluded.

I was totally taken aback, I knew I was being bought it was the only way to save the family estates but to be bought only to be made into a sissy husband was something that was unfathomable.

I asked to be excused and went back to my room to ponder this new circumstance.

As I closed the door to my room I was wondering what all this actually meant.

I made my way to my bed and reached to the dresser drawers, pulling out a sports magazine and flipping it open to a picture of a young man dressed in stockings and a bra, in front of another man with a big cock, the lipstick on the young man's lips was cherry red, and the woman standing next to the other man with the big cock had a caption on it "Fluff him up for me so he can fuck me". I reached down and my cock was rapidly hardening.

The next day I went to the dressing room and what I saw laid out for me was a pretty white dress there were some women there who were to assist me so I would appear proper the my new wife.

When they removed my clothes and noticed right away that I was clean shaven, they were rather surprised and moved on to doing my nails painting them in corresponding colors to what was being used for the ceremony. With my nails done they then pierced my ears with diamond studs that had a dangly end on them, then the plucking of the eyebrows and while I was laying on the bed, I felt someone playing with my cock or at least I thought it was playing, then it got quite uncomfortable and then a single click sound and I realized I was just put into chastity. I thought to myself, gee not even a last orgasm, shows how little concern she has for my own comfort or joy. I raised my hands as they slid the dress down over my shoulders and then they went about doing what they could with my not so long hair. The high heeled shoes came next and at least they gave me a chance to get used to them. It was then that one of them noticed they had forgotten to plug my ass, and it must have looked ludicrous as one of them had their hand up my dress trying to push this plug into my asshole. When they finally had it in place I had to learn how to walk in the high heeled shoes again. Then it was time.

As I entered the chapel and started my way down the aisle I was to everyone's surprise an amazingly beautiful bride. She was standing down at the front, dressed in a very masculine looking black leather evening gown, to think all of the people I had invited that was now looking at me in astonishment as they saw their male friend walking down the aisle in a wedding dress. I had even invited a few ex-girlfriend's to my marriage thinking they would be sad to see another good man out of the running. One of them leaned towards me as I walked by her and said. "If I had known you liked this we would have had such a better time of things then we did". It kind of made me think and then I was walking again and before I knew it I was facing my soon to be, I didn't even know what to call her. She was taller than I was and she looked down at me and obviously liked what she saw because she was smiling.

We both turned to the preacher who proceeded to begin the ceremony. When it came time for the vows they were a little different than I thought they would be.

He turned to me and said.

Do you take this woman, do you allow her to rule over you, to control you, to make you do what she wants. Do you understand that if she is cross with you she has the right to beat you until she is satisfied you will not do it again. Do you further allow her to have sexual relations with whomever she chooses and be willing to participate in these activities in any way that she seems fit for you to do. And lastly do you relinquish your manhood to her to control forever, to have yourself transformed into a woman to whatever degree that she sees fit at the time.

It took me a while to realize that I was giving up everything to a woman I didn't even know other then the fact that she shared a similar fetish that I enjoyed myself.

The room was deathly quiet waiting for my response.

"I do" I said.

She smiled greatly

Then the preacher turned to her.

Do you take this sissy to do with what you want?

"I do" she said.

The bells began to ring and we made our way down the aisle to the door and to the waiting car, she held the door open for me and as ducted inside and she scooted inside next to me. Then another man got into the car and sat down on the other side of me.

"I want you to know I am so happy to have you, I always knew you were already a sissy and ones who are broken by their own hand are always the best sissies to marry. " My new wife told me.

"Who is he" I asked.

"He is my lover, you don't think that I wasn't going to bring a man with a large cock on our honeymoon did you." She told me.

She motioned for the man and he undid his pants and pulled out a monster size cock.

"I want you to play with it get it nice and hard for me"

It was the first time I had ever touched a cock other than my own, and it was very big and thick. I took it in my hand and began to rub it up and down and felt it getting hard in my hand. By the time it was fully erect it must have been ten inches long and two inches thick.

"I hope you have that plug inside of you, because if I don't feel like it you may have to sit in for me and that monster will be going up your ass." She smiled at me.

She had the driver pull off on a dirt road, we all got out of the car and she instructed me to put do as she was doing which was laying on the hood of the car, she reached over and held my hand as our dresses were raised and my plug was removed and the man with the big cock took her, and the driver of the car popped my cherry, we both looked into each other's eyes and I realized our marriage was being consummated right here in the woods, she had such lovely eyes as the man took his time sliding his average size cock into my ass and my poor wife had that monster of cock inside of her but she was enjoying herself I could read that much. She leaned over and we kissed, so gently her lips were so soft and just a little tongue, it was truly like two girls kissing while be fucked.

It seemed like forever and at the same time it was over so quickly I heard the driver grunt and thrust deeply into my asshole and he shot his load deep inside of me. The man with the big cock took a little longer and when he came they were both screaming to heaven itself. Everyone tidied up a bit and we were back in the car and off to our honeymoon and to happier times I was certain.

□

Razors Edge

I am not sure why I did what I did, I obviously didn't think very much about it else I wouldn't have done it at all, I mean there was pretty much no way to hide it once the deed was done, but for some reason it never crossed my mind. You see I have been a secret cross dresser for most of my life, I always enjoyed the feeling of being naughty, you know wearing a pair of panties under my work clothes or maybe even stockings or pantyhose, it was great fun my mind would always be racing thinking someone is going to notice and my cock was always rock hard. It was such great fun at least it was for me, it seemed whenever the subject of cross dressing or anything to do with it ever came up whether it was with my friends, my wife, or people at work, they would always seem to think that those people were freaks or something, I never got it, it is just clothes, who is to say what one gender can or should wear over the other gender. I mean what I was doing was equivalent of my wife throwing my boxers on or wearing my dress shirt or something like that but nobody ever called a woman dressing in those things a freak; they always thought those things were hot or exciting. It seems we very much have a double standard when it comes to men wearing anything but what men are supposed to wear. It really is a shame if you ask me since the fact that most clothes for men out there are just drab and ugly, women have so much better choices when it comes to what to wear and that includes both under and outer wear.

Again I should have known that I was stepping over the line when I brought that razor up my leg and removed a swath of hair, I mean how would I explain why my legs were as smooth as my wives, it was obvious that she would eventually either see my legs or touch them and then the jig would be up and I would no longer be in the closet. What would she think of me, but for some reason those thoughts did not seem to make much headway in my brain as I brought the razor up my leg again and brilliant clean smooth skin appeared before me. I guess all I was thinking about was how good my legs would look in those sheer stockings I had tucked in the back of my briefcase. I had bought them a long time ago and quickly realized that it was difficult to imagine myself very feminine looking when I could see my leg hair through the stockings themselves, it wasn't very attractive. The immediate solution was to only buy opaque stockings this way the leg hair was quietly seethed in material and was not visible to the naked eye or at least my eye since I was the only one that ever saw my legs in stockings. Another swath of bare skin opened before my eyes and I realized I had committed myself to this activity and had no place to go but to finish it. I kept thinking about those sheet stockings and how exciting it would be to rubbing my cock through my panties with my legs up in the air clean and smooth as I ran my other hand up and down my leg. The right leg was completed front and back and it looked so amazing, I ran my hand down it and it felt wonderful, like I was seeing and feeling my leg for the first time. I quickly started on the left leg. The knock on the bathroom door startled me to know end, it was my wife asking if I was ok in there, I squeaked out a yes to her and heard her walk back out. I knew she had plans tonight and was going to need the shower herself soon, so I concentrated on getting done what I started quickly and accurately didn't want to cut my leg. Once both legs were smooth and clean of all hair I realized just how silly my hairy crotch looked and without much regard or thought for that matter I quickly made work of that and within minutes I was looking at my cock and balls like they were brand new and hairless I felt younger just touching them. I cleaned up and dried myself off and snuck back to the bedroom quickly getting dressed.

I watched my wife go into the bathroom and heard the shower turn on, I went and found my brief case and took out the sheet stockings and undid my pants and slid them on one leg at a time, the feeling was indescribable it was like the enjoyment of wearing stockings was now multiplied by one hundred. My legs were tingling and my cock was rock hard. Just to add to the fun I was going to have tonight I took out a pair of my wife's sexy lacy boy shorts and put them on. I don't usually wear my wife's underwear I go out and buy my own, but I had seen these in her drawer and I longed to wear them. Just as the elastic band snapped as I let go of them after pulling them above my hard cock, I heard the shower turn off. I quickly got my pants and shirt back on as my wife came out of the shower naked and dripping wet. She looked at me kind of funny like and asked me if everything was ok, I felt my heart sink a little and told her that everything was fine. I continued to fiddle with things about my shirt or get something out of the drawer and she put one leg up on the bed and put some lotion on it, she obviously shaved her legs as well, then the other leg was up on the bed exposing her cleanly shaved pussy.

Why don't you come over here and give me a kiss she told me. I smiled at her and made my way around the bed to her and I got closer and was leaning in to give her a kiss, she simply said oh not here pointing at the lips on her face and then down to her pussy. This was very out of context for her she was usually not so poignant about her desires. I was very much a submissive husband even if she didn't pick up on the obvious signs that I exhibited outwardly, and one of them was right here as I got down on my knees in front of her and began to kiss her clean and smooth lips. Now how about a little French kissing as I felt her hands on the back of my head and I began to push my tongue between her lips and further into her vagina, the smell of her perfumed soap was so sweet and intoxicating, she used her grip on my to angle my head so that my tongue was licking up more so I could flick her clitoris with my tongue, she liked it when I concentrated my efforts on her clitoris. I heard her say there that's the spot, with her legs open and apart my own hands came up and caressed her buttocks, it was so smooth and silky and for some odd reason I thought of the fact that my own buttocks was now just as smooth as hers. I could hear her breathing change a little and knew from her fingers digging into my hair that the first orgasm was soon to arrive; she removed one hand from my head and began to apply pressure right above where her crotch starts. She then told me to put two fingers inside of her and I did just that she was so wet my fingers slid inside of her, now I was concentrating on her clitoris full time not only licking it but sucking it into my mouth it was small but I for some reason thought of this as what it would be like to suck on a cock from this position. She then told me to curl my fingers upwards and to play with her G spot. Again I did just as she told me , I wasn't sure what she was trying to accomplish but it seemed like she had a very specific goal in mind, her breathing came in gasps and her pelvis was shaking or vibrating, the breathing then began to make a sound a low sound that was getting higher in pitch as she began to gyrate and shake it was becoming harder to keep my tongue on her clit as she the moan was now more like a shrill, the hand that was still on my head quickly left its position which caused me to release my hold on her clit with my mouth, as I moved back her hand came quickly to her pussy and she vigorously began to masturbate herself while screaming out yes yes yes, then oh my god, then yes yes yes again. She came in a way that I had never seen her cum before and in an amazing turn of events she ejaculated all over me, I had her cum on my face on my shirt and quite a bit of it on my pants as the dark spots materialized from the soaking I just took. She collapsed on the bed with her hand still gently caressing her pussy. She turned to me and said now that's what I am talking about, that was amazing, you did a wonderful job licking my pussy, in fact I have to admit you lick pussy just like a woman would lick pussy I am the luckiest woman of them all for having you. I stood up and smiled at her and she then pointed to my pants and told me that I better change those. I looked down in horror realizing that I changed my pants now she would see me in my stockings and her own panties and this perfect start to an evening would be ruined and could end up with me in divorce court if she reacted badly to me wearing stockings and panties. I saw the stain on my pants and was like it will dry these should be ok. She laughed at me and told me not to be silly go change we still have time before the girls get here. Aren't you going to get dressed I asked her, and she smiled and said that she wanted to see my hard cock before she put her clothes on. It was then that I realized that I was stuck between a rock and a hard place, if I refused she would be concerned and if I removed my pants then it would be out in the open that I was something else besides a loving husband, she would probably think of me as a freak or a pervert or something.

Is everything ok honey, is something wrong, she asked me I told her everything was fine. She smiled at me and leaned on her elbow like I was going to put on a show for her or something. Come on my lover let me see that hard cock she growled at me. I was taken a back again this was so not in her character to be this aggressive, she was usually more of the whatever you want to do honey type person.

Then her face changed to more of an inquisitive look, and she asked me if I was trying to hide something from her, and I laughed and told her what do I have to hide from my loving wife I asked. She smiled again and told me to take my pants off or she would come over here and take them off for me.

I undid the snap and tried again to talk my way out of it, and this time she scotted over and sat on the edge of the bed right in front of me. What happened next I still to this day could not have believed in a thousand years? She looked up at me and asked if I was scared to show her how pretty I must look in stockings and panties especially now that I had finally shaved my legs. I was speechless, I am pretty sure my mouth dropped open when I heard her say those words.

Did you think that I did not know about your stocking and panty fetish sweetheart? She asked me. I have known for quite some time, I had been waiting to see how long it would take you until you did shave your legs, because I knew that if you did that it was more than just a thing it was something inside of you and then and only then would I be able to accept it openly. When I got in the shower and saw the hair you missed by the drain and then saw it on the razor I was so happy to know that you had finally committed to it and that I could finally openly accept it. She told me.

I am so happy honey, it is going to be so much easier on you from now on, you can wear whatever feminine attire you want to around the house, out of the house, to work whatever you feel you are comfortable with. If you want we can paint your toes, maybe pierce your ears it is all up to you now, no more reason to hide it from me or the world.

When my pants were lowered like it was the opening of some big gala or something, she did get pissed that I was wearing her panties. Now sweetheart, I don't mind you wearing panties but don't you ever take my panties again do you understand you can go out and buy your own panties. The panties were pulled down and my hard cock came out and she took it into her mouth and it was the most amazing feeling having my first blowjob while wearing stockings, and she took full advantage of that, and with my dick in her mouth her hands began to run up and down my sheer stockings it was the most amazing feeling in the world. Needless to say it wasn't long before I was shooting my load into her mouth, and evidently it was a large amount as some of it was dribbling down the side of her mouth as she stood back up to face me. She took her finger and pushed the dribble back into her mouth, her red lips were so hot looking when she did that and then she leaned over and kissed me and I quickly learned that she hadn't swallowed it at all and there in the bedroom standing in front of my wife with panties and stockings on after the best blowjob I had ever received I learned something else about my wife, she was far more kinkier then I had originally thought as I felt her tongue slide into my mouth with my load of cum still sitting right there on top of her tongue, and then it was in my mouth and I tasted myself on my own tongue and then it was gone as I swallowed my first load of cum ever in my life and at the bequest of my own wife. It was all so much to take in so quickly but she smiled at me and told me there would be plenty more of that plus a whole lot more of a whole lot more. She got dressed for her evening out with her friends and I got dressed for an evening in front of the computer writing the story of what happened this evening.

When the doorbell rang I got up and let her three friends into the house, they were all dressed hot, I mean these ladies looked like they were dressed to kill this evening, and when my wife came out of the bedroom she was also dressed in similar fashion. They all embraced and she was all smiles and I wasn't sure why and then she simply began telling them about the orgasm that I had given to her and how she was finally able to ejaculate they were all very excited to hear about this evidently this was something they had all been working on for some time clandestinely, and then she continued to inform them that was only the icing on the cake, when she thoroughly had their attention and my own as well, she informed them that I was now officially out and was openly wearing panties and stockings. I probably should have put something on other than sweat pants and in one swoop my wife had my sweat pants down around my ankles and the girls were all smiling and pointing at my panties and stockings. The odd thing was they weren't laughing they were all so excited just like my wife. I was able to get my pants up again, and I could hear them saying how wonderful it was, that this was great news indeed. I heard one of them saying how this was such a good first step and I wasn't sure I understood what she meant by that, but soon they were making their goodbyes and now unlike before they all came over and hugged me and kissed me on the lips to say goodbye like I had become one of them part of the tribe or something, one of them even caressed my cock through my sweat pants right in front of my wife who not only saw but gave me a sexy grin about it.

Then they were out the door for their evening of fun and I sat on the couch and tried to make sense of it all, it was an amazing evening that was for sure, I just wasn't quite sure where it was all headed.

☐

Telling the Wife

The day that I opened up to my wife about wearing panties and stockings was the scariest day of my life; I had no idea how she was going to react to the whole thing at all.
The fact that she found it acceptable was even more astonishing to me, in all the articles I had read the majority of women have a lot of issues in accepting the cross dressing habits of the men who love them.
She had me bring out all of my panties and stockings and display them in front of her.
"Honey if you are going to do this then we have to do this right, and she picked out a few of the panties and stockings and simply threw them in the trash."
"If my man is going to be a sissy, then the least he can be is a well-dressed sissy."
With that she got up and went back to her day. I was left to clean up my now dubbed sissy clothing and put it back hidden in the closet.
As I was lifting the box back up to the top shelf way in the back of the closet I turned to see her standing in the doorway.
"What do you think you are doing?" she asked
"I was putting my sissy clothing away" I told her.
"Oh no, that is out in the open now so you go find room in your drawers for them, I suggest you start throwing away some of what is already in your sock and underwear drawers because you certainly are not going to be wearing those much anymore. Maybe they should go in a box and in the back of the closet you are out honey you might as well get used to it."
She informed me.

I simply stared at her as she turned and left me holding my panties and stockings box. I had that feeling deep down inside that what I thought of as just an everyday now and then type of thing was now becoming something a little bit more.

The morning preceded pretty much normal after that, we were going to the flea market for some shopping and I grabbed my jacket and was walking to the front door where my wife was and she stopped me at the door.

"Are you wearing your panties and stockings my little sissy?" she asked.

I gave her a weird look and told her that I wasn't

"Well you can march you little sissy ass back into the bedroom and get changed because we are not going anywhere unless you have your little panties and stockings on." She told me.

I was taken a little aback at her enthusiasm and slinked back into the bedroom to change.

I had to admit it was a little different putting on panties and stockings knowing my wife was waiting for me. My cock was rock hard when I snapped my jeans closed and made my way back to the door.

"Well look at that the little sissy has a hard on, you really do like wearing panties and stockings don't you, oh we are going to have so much fun with this." She said.

The flea market was always crowded and we usually just did some window shopping grabbed a bite to eat and call it a day. This time however the wife kept finding all these little sexy clothing stalls and went into each one. Of course I followed right behind her, she looked at all types of things, sexy skirts and dresses, every once and awhile holding one up to me to see if she thought it might fit. This embarrassed me and I must have blushed bright red.

My wife tapped the attendant and said.

"Oh look see my little sissy is embarrassed."

And then asked the attendant.

"Do you think this hot little dress would fit him?"

The attendant explained that it seemed like a good match and if he wanted to try it on he could use the dressing room in the back.

My wife thought about it for a minute or two and then handed me the dress and told me to go try it on.

I gave her a look of sheer terror but she was insistent and I found myself walking into the back of a very busy flea market to try on a sexy hot dress. When the little curtain closed behind me I felt like I was in a foreign country, I fumbled with my own clothes and when my pants fell to the floor I realized my stockings were now visible to the rest of the people in the stall.

I heard my wife as I stepped out of my pants.

"Oh sweet heart you did choose a very nice pair of stockings to wear today."

When I didn't respond she continued.

"When someone pays you a compliment it is best if you respond to them else you might find yourself in a very embarrassing situation or maybe even need to be punished, or maybe even both.

The cold chill that shot up my spine was all too real.

"Thank you Ma'am" I said loud enough for everyone to hear.

"That's much better." She responded.

It took me a little bit to figure out the in's and out's of getting the dress on my body and when I informed my wife that I had it on, the front curtain simply opened completely and my wife and the attendant were standing there.

"Oh look he is embarrassed again." My wife laughed

The attendant also smiled and informed my wife that it fit quite well and that with the purchase of the dress it also came with fishnet stockings and some crotch less underwear.

As I was standing there in the dressing room my wife completed the deal and asked me if I wanted to wear the dress home or if I would like to get changed into your old clothes. It was then I realized that she was holding my clothes, not sure when or how she got them but I realized that she could simply walk away and I would be left having to make my way around in this dress.

There was that cold chill again.

If I had a camera the look on my wife's face would have been a picture of pure evil as she knew that she held all the cards in her hands and the smile was that of one who knows they are now the Master.

I knew I had to be careful here.

"I would prefer to wear the clothes I came in for now, I would like to get used to these new clothing items prior to be seen in public with them." I said to her meekly.

"Well said she told me, because you will wear these clothes when I want you too, but I agree you are not ready yet to be seen in public with me, like I said before if we are going to do this then we need to do it right."

As I stepped out of the dressing room in my regular manly clothes I knew that my life had changed in a big way.

We stopped at a few other places and now that my wife had some idea of the size I was didn't require me to try anything else on for her, she picked out some shape wear that would make my butt and hips look bigger and more womanly. She did need a little help with the bra fitting, which was to some degree more embarrassing then the trying on the sexy dress. The attendant measured me right there in front of the stall for all to see.

This was the thing that I couldn't get over, was the fact that the attendant's didn't seem to really care that these things were being bought for a man, in fact the more I looked around the more I realized that nobody really cared, either that or they were too busy just trying to get the things done that they were there for. Either way it kind of made me relax, well that was until some redneck walked past me while the woman held one of the bra's to my chest and explained about how to choose a cup size for me and I heard the words "Faggot" in my ears. It caught me off guard and I realized that even in our very accepting society there would always be people who had a little extra time in their busy day to take a moment and demonstrate just how intolerant they are about others. I let it go as the attendant handed my wife a plastic bag with my new Bra in it, I had never owned a bra, but then again I also never owned a dress before either.

She seemed to take her time in the stalls that held shoes, pumps of all shapes and sizes, I had to admit the shoes were very sexy looking, I had always thought about shoes but felt that I would be too scared to try them on which had to be done to make sure they fit. However with my wife here it seemed so much easier to shop for women's clothes when you have a woman there with you, maybe that was why the attendants were being so helpful, maybe when you have a woman involved in your cross dressing that others don't just think of you as a freak or a pervert, but an actual person. Maybe they think with the woman involved that the dressing would be done with better taste. All these thoughts just kept running through my mind.

"Step into these"

I came back from drifting off to find my wife placing two pumps on the floor for me to step into. They were a high gloss black and had a four inch heel on them, I liked the fact that they also had ankle straps, the act of being strapped into your shoes just seemed so hot to me. I was very happy when they fit quite nicely being four inches taller made me quite tall, but the smile on my wife's face was so beautiful as I stepped out of them. She obviously must have seen me light up when I had them on and told the lady that we would take the black and red ones.

The next shop we stopped in didn't sell female clothing at all, in fact it only sold sex videos and sex toys, this made me nervous again, but my wife assured me it was all part of the experience.

I followed behind her as she went to the table that had butt plugs on it and she picked them up examined them and eventually chose three of them. When I asked what she was planning to do with them, she simple shushed me.

"You know damn well where these are going to go."

Then she was looking at strap ons.

"Honey I don't know if that is something......"

"Dear it isn't always about what you want, you want to dress like a girl and I am fine with that, hell I am really turned on by it, but one of the things I have always wanted was a penis, and now you have given me the chance to have one and to use it as well." She told me.

I simply swallowed and watch her put down the one she had and picked up an even bigger one.

"I suggest you accept this, I am sure you will come to like it." While holding the large strap on, I watched her hand touch the one that was even bigger than the one she had in her hands already.

I simply nodded my head.

"Good little sissy" she smiled.

The rest of the time at the flea market was uneventful and we finally made our way back home with bags in hand.

She immediately took the bags to the bedroom while I got online to answer some emails.

A few minutes later I heard her calling my name and when I came out of the computer room I saw her standing there in our bedroom door.

She was naked except for the fact that she was wearing the large strap on she had just purchased.

"I have changed into my new things, I think it is time for you to change into your new things."

I knew I had a choice here, but at the same time I knew which choice I would make, my cock had been hard all day long and it was hard right now looking at my wife a very large cock especially knowing where she wanted to put her new cock.

I walked past her and into the bedroom to change into my new dress and lose my anal virginity.

But that is another story…..

□

A Note from the Author

Well here it is the end of another project, I get mixed feelings
when I come to the end of a project, I enjoy writing so much
that I am sad to be at the end but at the same time I know that
now others will get a chance to experience my wonderful
lustful and sometimes sadistic thoughts via the story or the
assignment. I just have so much fun writing about the
experiences I have with my own submissive play things or
even when it is just a fantasy that grows in my head, we like
to think of those as things to be experienced at a later date.
So now it is your turn to once again do what I ask of you.
I would like to hear from you, I am going to give you my
personal email address so you can contact me so that I can get
your feedback on the stories and the assignments and
anything else you would like to tell me about. I would love to
hear about your own stories and experiences, I just love it
when I get email from the people who read my work, so don't
hesitate to contact me, and I always make it a point to write
back.

Write to me soon…….

Love

Mistress Jessica

Mistressjessica01@gmail.com